De Ingenium Humanus (About the Innate Characteristics of Humans)

Book 3: Ethical Deceit and Moral Deception

Rivadeneyra of Phoenix

Contents

Purpose

The purpose of this argument is to explain the utility of Ethical Deceit and Moral Deception. We maintain the great populace of humanity is incorrect in their statements regarding truth. For not only is it in ones benefit to deceive others but it is also in ones benefit to deceive themselves. We will endeavor to explain this by means of an explanation of truth. We will also make sure to explain why we as humans need to be truthful.

Explicit Meaning of Expression

The meaning of expression is the very subject upon which all arguments are dependent. The expression of ideas occurs in various forms the most common of which is in words. Even our very thoughts come to us be means of words. In the same manner we may say truth resides in our expression of it. That is not to say truth is purely expression but it is to say the truth which we know of and may strive for will be shared by means of our expression. As stated by Rabindranath Tagore:

> *"Things are distinct not in their essence but in their appearance; in other words, in their relation to one to whom they appear. This is art, the truth of which is not in substance or logic, but in expression."*

Note; we are not saying there is no absolute truth. We hold there is an absolute truth to which all honest expressions aspire to. While it may be admitted an absolute truth does exist it must also be stated an expression in contradiction to absolute truth is not necessarily a deceptive expression as the expression is not deceptive unless intended to be so (actus non facit reum nisi mens sit rea; *the act is not guilty unless the mind is guilty*). Similarly we must also state the lack of expression may be deemed an expression just as the lack of taking action is an action. As such the lack of expression may be deceptive or honest as any expression may be.

We must make mention of the potentiality of an expression to be an honest expression but to not be a truthful expression in comparison with the absolute truth. At present we recognize the human species or any other entity for that matter may only express what they understand to be the truth. That is to say at best we may only give an honest expression. We may endeavor that our honest expression is in accordance with absolute truth, but our honest expression may not succeed in achieving the level of accord we intend. Indeed we must presently admit we may perceive of the truth but be unable to express it, though we may express as best we can which we perceive. As such it may not be said our honest expression of what we perceive is false though it may be stated it is not an absolutely true expression of what we perceived. So it is stated by one Kahil Gibran:

"The reality of the other person lies not in what he reveals to you, but what he cannot reveal to you. Therefore, if you would understand him, listen not to what he says, but rather to what he does not say."

Expressions are manifested in various ways the most common of which is words. Words are commonly constructed of both phonic and symbolic definitions. We do recognize words my exist simply phonically and not symbolically such as the words of some of the great tribes of the Americas or words may exist symbolically but not phonically such as the words expressed by means of sign language. None the less we do recognize words at minimum must be manifested phonically or symbolically and are commonly manifest in both modes.

Great effort is taken by the scope of humanity to define the meaning of words. It must be assumed such effort is taken in order to route out truth by guarding against deceit. By agreeing upon fixed terms for words we decrease the amount of ambiguity each word has. The degradation of ambiguity gives rise to certainty or confidence. This certainty is taken as truth, but only literary truth or analytical truth. That is to say truth by meaning of the words. This literary or analytic truth is what we call the explicit meaning of words. As stated by Plato and Confucius:

"The beginning of wisdom is the definition of terms"

And

> *"If language is not correct, then what is said is not what is meant; if what is said is not what is meant, then what must be done remains undone; if this remains undone, morals and art will deteriorate; if justice goes astray, the people will stand about in helpless confusion. Hence there must be no arbitrariness in what is said. This matters above everything."*

The explicit meaning of words is the agreed upon definition of words. The explicit meaning of words may be discerned simply by means of a dictionary or by the commonly intended meaning of a word in speech. Context must be considered in determining the explicit meaning of words. As observed in the dictionary or in speech one word may have multiple agreed upon definitions. The utilization of one definition as opposed to another is dependent upon the context of the word. It is to be noted that the explicit meaning of words is what we observe as varying form culture to culture. For the explicit meaning of words is tied to the word itself in a given context. That is to say is tied to the phonic and/or symbolic expression of the word.

We may endeavor to state the explicit meaning of words and thus of language is the meaning derived from the common expression of the words. It must be said by us the means of expression are limited only by the variations upon which we associate meaning to any given sound, symbol, or combination of the two. As such we would state the variation of explicit expression is nearly limitless. That is to say due to the various combinations which may be utilized to make an explicit expression there an infinite assortment of languages may exist. For example here is a listing of the symbolic expression of smile from various languages:

smile [smail] noun
an act of smiling, or the resulting facial expression
Example: `How do you do?' he said with a smile; the happy smiles of the children

Arabic:	إبْتِسامم، تَبسُم	*Japanese:*	微笑
Chinese (Simplified):	微笑，喜色	*Korean:*	미소, 환한 웃음
Chinese (Traditional):	微笑，喜色	*Latvian:*	smaids
Czech:	Úsměv	*Lithuanian:*	šypsena
Danish:	Smil	*Norwegian:*	smil
Dutch:	Glimlach	*Polish:*	uśmiech
Estonian:	Naeratus	*Portuguese (Brazil):*	sorriso
Finnish:	Hymy	*Portuguese (Portugal):*	sorriso
French:	Sourire	*Romanian:*	zâmbet, surâs
German:	das Lächeln	*Russian:*	Улыбка
Greek:	Χαμόγελο	*Slovak:*	Úsmev
Hungarian:	Mosoly	*Slovenian:*	Nasmeh
Icelandic:	Bros	*Spanish:*	Sonrisa
Indonesian:	Senyuman	*Swedish:*	Leende
Italian:	Sorriso	*Turkish:*	Gülümseme

While we do presently state languages, which are explicitly expressed, are infinite we must also state what is expressed by those infinite languages is not infinite. We must state the explicit meaning of what is expressed is confined to our experiences. Be those experience actual events which we ourselves have endured of imaginary experiences which we have imagined we may not state that we may express anything which we do not perceive or conceive of. As such it may be said our content of expression is limited to the conditions of our existence, an existence encompassing both actual existence and imaginary existence, the former of which is the reality, the latter of which is an illusion created by an entity which resides in the reality.

It is to be noted that we are including all aspects of our being in our expression of experience. We are not diverging between physical experience, psychological experience, emotional experience, and any other type of experience we fail to make mention of here. We seek only to state anything which we endeavor to express is something we have experienced and do not seek to get bogged down in an argument regarding what we may experience or if what we experience is real or not.

Now we recognize an expression is either a physical action with a specific meaning, that is to say a physical expression or body language. Or an expression is the summation and interaction of words, that is to say a literal expression. We find the explicit meaning of an expression is simply the combination of the explicit value of the actions or words which it consists of and the proper interaction of those actions or words with one another in a given context.

Any expression that is not a nonsensical expression is an honest explicit expression. For an expression to make sense the actions or words which construct it must fit together. As an example if someone were to laugh at something humorous we would say their expression of laughter was explicitly honest. However if they were to laugh as they were being tortured we would find this response very perplexing and nonsensical, we would consider the expression to be explicitly deceitful. That is to say we would construe they were hiding how they really felt about being tortured. As another example if we were to say, "The oceans are a lovely yellow", we observe the expression is explicitly honest for the words interact properly with one another and are being used in the proper manner. At the same time if we were to say, "Yellow lovely a are oceans the", we observe this expression is not explicitly honest due to the improper interaction of the words.

Thus we state every language will have actions or words whether they are expressed phonically or symbolically. The actions/words will be given agreed upon explicit meanings or definitions by the society using them. The same society will construct rules of how the actions/words are to be combined in the formation of expressions. The agreed upon explicit meaning of the actions/words or definitions in conjunction with one another in adherence with the rules governing the proper formation of expressions, as agreed upon by the same society will give rise to explicit honesty. So expressed by Miguel Cervantes:

"By such innovations are languages enriched, when the words are adopted by the multitude, and naturalized by custom."

We do presently avoid any descriptions of rules which govern a particular language. It is our intention to describe the explicit meaning of words and expressions as well as explicit honesty of expressions and languages. As such we do not limit ourselves to any particular word, expression, or language but are indeed referring to all words, expressions, and languages. Our analysis is to include phonic, literate, symbolic, and physical words, expressions, and languages.

Implicit Meaning of Expression

It may not be said words, expressions, and languages are devoid of any other meaning then their explicit meaning. To say such a thing would be in definite contradiction to our everyday experiences with words, expressions, and languages. In fact as expressed by us the explicit meaning of words was determined as the agreed upon meaning of the word in an effort to decrease the ambiguity of the word when used. This implies there is a meaning to words upon which the explicit meaning is derived. Indeed such is the case.

The purpose of words, expressions, and languages will be discussed later in the Purpose of Expression section, but for the moment we will state it is to convey the self. We do not specify who the self is conveyed to for we may convey the self to the self by means of words, expressions, and languages. To convey the self to the self is what we may call thought, reflection, realization, self perception, and so on. We may also convey the self to that which is not the self. That is to say we may convey the self to the external world. Expression of the self to the external world is what we may refer to as speech, demeanor, action, and any other external indicators of the self.

In either case we affirm the goal of words, expressions, and languages is to convey the self either to the self or to that which is not the self. This intention to express the self encompasses all which are part of the self. That is to say we intend to express is our ethical self, our moral self, our psychological self, our physical self, our meta-physical self, and any other definition of the self we fail to mention but have been expressed or will be expressed throughout the course of human conception and realization.

This expression of the self is what we refer to as the implicit meaning of words, expressions, and languages. The implicit meaning is what we mean or intend to express to our own self or to others. It is the implied meaning of what we say. More will be discussed in regards to the establishment of our intention when speaking. For the time being suffice to say what we intend to say is what we wish the implicit recipient to grasp. We will give more explanation on the implicit recipient in the Implicit Recipient of Expressions section.

Presently we must state the aforementioned explicit meaning of expression is derived from the implicit meaning of expression. Previously, we stated the explicit meaning of expression is the agreed upon social definition of an expression. This agreed upon definition is generally the consensus of the application of said expression to facilitate a specific implicit meaning. That is to say we came to agree a certain expression has a certain meaning because when the majority of us wished to express this aspect of ourselves we consistently utilized the same expression.

For example we associate the expression of a smile with the implicit meaning of joy of some type. Be this joy a physical joy, that is to say pleasure, an emotional joy or happiness, or a psychological joy, that is to say elation. The implicit meaning of a smile is a response to joy. The commonality of the expression of a smile across the species when the species is experiencing some form of joy grants us the opportunity to rid the expression of a smile of its ambiguities and create a fixed explicit meaning or definition, such as stated by Webster's Online Dictionary:

> *Main Entry:* ^{2}*smile*
> *Function: noun*
> *Date: 15th century*
> *1 : a facial expression in which the eyes brighten and the*

> *corners of the mouth curve slightly upward and which ex-*
> *presses especially amusement, pleasure, approval, or some-*
> *times scorn*
> *2 : a pleasant or encouraging appearance*

It was expressed by us earlier while there are infinite languages or infinite modes of explicit expression may come into existence, the explicit meaning is finite. The limit of the explicit meaning is in actuality limited by the implicit meaning. The implicit meaning may only be derived from our experience be they actual or imaginary. As such the explicit meaning being the common implicit meaning of a given word, expression, or language becomes finite due to the finite experiences we may actual have or imagine.

Above is the English explicit expression of the human phenomena of showing joy by means of contortion of the face, the explicit meaning and explicit expression as it is defined by the English speaking population referred to as a smile. Similarly there is an equivalent explicit expression with an equivalent explicit meaning derived from the very same implicit meaning in other languages. For example the word smile of course has an equivalent in other languages such as Spanish, as found at Diccionarios.com:

> *sonrisa*
>
> **nombre femenino**
> *Gesto de alegría, felicidad o placer que se hace curvando la*
> *boca hacia arriba como si se fuese a reír, pero levemente y*
> *sin emitir ningún sonido:*

Thus it may be said the explicit meaning of words, expressions, and languages is the implicit meaning of words, expressions, and languages assigned to a common explicit expression. In any given language the explicit meaning of any aspect of an expression may be determined by the implicit meaning for the common explicit expression used to express the implicit meaning in question. As is shown below in the following equation defining explication, where $\bar{E}_E$ is the average explicit expressions used, M_I is the implicit meaning meant by all of the expressions used, and M_E is the explicit meaning of the expression assigned to the expression due to the commonality of the expression being used to express the implied meaning in question:

$$M_E = \bar{E}_E / M_I$$

(Math Note: For those who question why the explicit meaning is defined in terms of a ratio what we seek to express is the explicit meaning is always in relation to the implicit meaning. At best the explicit meaning may be the same as the implicit meaning. Otherwise the explicit meaning is some partial variation of the implicit meaning. It must also be recognized the explicit meaning is in relation to the average explicit expression not the particular explicit expression. Recognition of this is essential as the fallacy in the following formulas is in the attempt to derive the implicit meaning from a particular explicit expression in a relation of the explicit meaning.)

This being the case one must wonder why we need to consider both explicit and implicit meanings. Why do we simply not operate by the implicit meaning since the explicit is simply the common implicit meaning? The answer is though the explicit meaning is the common implicit meaning, the words, expressions, and languages in question may express a variant implicit meaning that is not the common meaning and thus is not in agreement with the explicit meaning. This may be termed the process of implication.

Thus at best an implication or implicit meaning derived from an explicit expression used and the explicit meaning associated to that expression will approximate the actual implicit meaning. If the best case does occur it will occur as the particular explicit expression used approaches the average explicit expression used. Such convergence will not necessarily yield the best case scenario but we stipulate the best case scenario when it does occur will have the convergence of the particular expression to that of the average expression present. At worst implication or the derived implicit meaning will in no way be similar to the actual implicit meaning of what was expressed due to the particular explicit expression not approaching the average explicit expression, as shown by the equations below:

$$M_I \approx E_E / M_E \text{ (Best case where } E_E \approx \text{ or } = \bar{E}_E)$$

Or

$$M_I \neq E_E / M_E \text{ (Worse case where } E_E \neq \bar{E}_E)$$

It is the manner in which the incongruence of explicit meaning and implicit meaning occur that gives rise to honesty, deceit, deception, and misunderstanding. It must be noted that misunderstanding is not the same as deceit or deception. We will explain this in more detail in the Intent of Expression and Understanding sections. Indeed we must say misunderstanding is to deceit and deception as manslaughter is to murder. The former a negative act which was unintended and the latter an intended negative act.

Just as with explicit honesty there is implicit honesty. However unlike explicit honesty which was defined by the proper utilization of the explicit meaning and explicit mode of expression, implicit honesty is dependent upon our intention. For something to be implicitly honest at minimum we must intend to express our true self as best we can to the implicit recipient. So long as we endeavor to express honestly to the implicit recipient than we are implicitly honest though we may be misunderstood or are being deceitful when expressing externally such as being dishonest to convey the truth.

To not endeavor to express the self honestly most often results in deceit or deception. In the case of the former to the external is to be deceitful and for the latter to not express honestly to the self is to be deceptive. We must make note here to say it is entirely possible to not express the self honestly and to still be overtly honest. This statement, along with the conditions for overall honesty, deceit, deception, and understanding will be dealt with in the Intent of Expression Section and the Understanding Section.

When we make an expression; devoid of an honest implicit expression, than there is no implicit meaning of our expression. When such cases occur it is the intention of the expresser the meaning of what is expressed be solely the explicit meaning and to not have any implicit meaning. This is most notably the case of moral deception or the deception of the self. It is common for there to be a lack of any implicit meaning when practicing ethical deceit as well. We must state commonly when ethical deceit has an intended implicit recipient that recipient assuredly is not to be the intended explicit recipient. More will be expressed in regards to this in The Implicit Recipient of Expression section.

Purpose of Expression

We must now go back and recant the purpose of expression. We made an assumption regarding expressions purpose to true expression of our person and built upon that expression our foundation of explicit and implicit. Much has been written about the purpose of expression. While we make no denial expressions are used to deceive we do presently state the initial purpose of expressions is not of deception but of honesty.

Let us presuppose the purpose of expression is dishonesty. It is common for people to use expression for deceit and deception as well as for honesty. If we presume the purpose of expression is to dishonesty, that is to say to ethical deceit and moral deception we may determine if this assertion is true. Such an assumption is not simply mere speculation. For indeed we recognize there are those in this world who seek to benefit by deceit and deception. So stated by Dionysius Cato:

> *"The same words conceal and declare the thoughts of men."*

Upon exercising our presumption we must immediately recognize in order to be dishonest we must know the honest expression so we may avoid expressing it in its entirety. We have expressed earlier and will reiterate now that dishonesty does incorporate honesty within it specifically in regards to explicit honesty which must be present for our expression to avoid being nonsensical.

Similarly we must recognize what is dishonest or honest is an expression of what we perceive, conceive, or imagine. That is to say we are limited in what we may express by our very own perception, conception, or imagination; for as we have said earlier it is not possible for the self to express something which is beyond the aforementioned aspects of the self. We are not capable of expressions for things which we have no experience with.

Indeed were we to express an oddity or some creature which has never been experienced by our person or by the recipient to whom we speak we find our expression of it will right away attach itself to something which we do have experiences as. We will construct a simile, metaphor, or anthropomorphic association to something which is known to describe that which we have never described before.

Though it cannot be said either our association will suffice to give a true account of that which we seek to express we may state it will most likely state an honest account, but to what purpose. Why is it our expression is likely an honest expression? Simply because to make effort to express dishonestly when effort is not needed is a waste of our time, our effort, and our person.

To endeavor to express dishonestly what others have no perception, conception, or imagination of is futile at best. Indeed we would say to say nothing was just as effective if not more so when it comes to the expression of that which is not perceived, conceived, or imagined by the recipient of our expression than to exert the effort required to construct a falsity.

While we presupposed our purpose of expression is to be dishonest we see to express dishonestly continuously is utter futility. The requirements of our dishonestly, that is to say our desire to not reveal honestly, may be met equally with our silence as it may be met with our efforts of dishonest expression. To make no expression at all is to leave others to make conjectures, while some of those conjectures may be accurate without confirmation they will not be reliable, if not reliable than not assured, if not assured than potential dishonest, if potential dishonest than treated as dishonest. So stated by Robert Louis Stevenson:

> *"The cruelest lies are often told in silence. A man may have sat in a room for hours and not opened his mouth, and yet come out of that room a disloyal friend or a vile calumniator."*

Hence we state to be dishonest is easy to be honest hard. For honesty demands not only the expression of our person but an understanding of the recipient of our expression to such an extent that we may endeavor to not only express what we sought to express but to augment our expression in such a manner as to be sensible to the recipient of our expression. Such are the issues of first encounters between individuals, nations, cultures, or other species. When one meets with another, should they even communicate by the same means they will most assuredly be taxed to first come to a sufficient understanding of each other so as to communicate effectively. The expresser must understand the recipient in order for the recipient to come to understand the expresser.

The Explicit Recipient of Expression

What of the recipient of expression? We have made mention of this entity several times and have even alluded to the fact there is an implicit and explicit recipient which may not be the same entity. To give the short definition the recipient of expression is the being we intend to receive our expression. Be it our dishonest or honest expression. That being may be internal or external as well.

Our explicit expression may have many recipients some who are intended and others not intended. As such the explicit recipient of our expression may only be expressed in terms that would allow for an intended recipient and for unintended recipients. So we must state the explicit recipient may be any being whom is capable of receiving the explicit expression. That is to say any being within range, with the ability to perceive the explicit expression, and with the ability to comprehend the explicit expression is an explicit recipient.

While we do presently admit any being within range, with the ability to perceive, and comprehend the explicit expression is an explicit recipient we must affirm the explicit recipients will commonly understand the explicit expression in the same way. Such is our definition of the explicit meaning when extended to the explicit recipient. For the explicit meaning to be the agreed upon common meaning of an expression it must be assigned a common interpretation by the majority of the culture in which the expression exists.

We may not affirm the interpretation of the expression in any given society is an absolute for we are not aware of the explicit meaning of the expression to every possible being present. For as it was stated by us social variables such as different cultures, genders, species, and so forth may cause a different interpretation of the same sound and any number of those social variables may be present in the society as well. We may endeavor to say the expression when interpreted among a specific society will have a fixed and agreed upon definition.

We have previously stated in our section regarding Ethical Categorization and Moral Definition that social groups are commonly formed based on similarities existing among those who exist within the society in question. Admittedly we again recognize the similarity may not be necessarily tied to an ascribed status but may be connected to an acquired status such as common history shared in the region where the society is located. Thus there may be varying explicit meanings to terms used in the society in question; however it is assured there is an explicit meaning in said society accepted by the majority of said societal members.

Such an example is really an exception to the rule which we wish to provide. We make mention of it so others will not. We may limit the amount of variation by confining our social variables to be consistent for our comparison. But to do so would be divergent from the realistic situation the majority if not all societies are in now; that is to say social constructs consisting of various social variables, which may or may not contain specific dominant variables. As such we must admit it is probable nearly all members of the society will interpret the explicit meaning of the expression the same but we may not say absolutely this will be the case.

We make our assertion on the assumption those within a given society have had enough contact with others within their society but of divergent social variable as to have at least a rudimentary understanding of how their expression will be interpreted by the recipient in question or of the common meaning of the expression when used by the expresser in question. This rudimentary understanding is essential for the society to be constructed as a single society. Without the rudimentary understanding we do not have a single society consisting of divergent social variables. Rather we have two distinct societies unable to communicate with one another at present until they gain a rudimentary understanding of one another. Such is the sentiment expressed by Robert M Hutchins in regards to national communities and Jeremy Bentham in regards to individuals which comprise a nation:

> *"A world community can only exist with world communication, which means… common understanding, a common tradition, common ideas and common ideals."*

And

> *"It is vain to talk of the interest of the community, without understanding what is the interest of the individual"*

Emphasis is to be made to state our understanding of other members of our society of divergent social variables may be at minimum rudimentary but absolutely necessary. Such is explained in our previous chapter regarding Ethical Categorization and Moral Definition. While our understanding may transcend rudimentary such transcendence is not necessary for the formation of a society. Rudimentary understanding is necessary for a society for no single society may consist of beings which may not communicate with one another on at least a base level.

The Implicit Recipient of Expression

The implicit recipient may be defined as the recipient to receive the honest implied meaning of what is expressed. That is to say the implicit recipient shall receive the implied meaning of our expression; our honest implicit expression. Earlier we expressed the implicit meaning is what we seek to truly express, hence the implicit recipient may be defined as our true recipient or as the recipient whom we wish to communicate our self to.

Presently we recognize there are also unintended implicit recipients. We must state while the unintentional explicit recipient is acceptable and often beneficial the unintentional implicit recipients are not acceptable to us. To the extent minimal effort is exercised to avoid the former and great effort is utilized to avoid the latter.

It may be said we are willing to have unintentional explicit recipients for they would corroborate what was expressed; that is to say they will corroborate a specific audio or symbolic expression was used which contains a specified agreed upon explicit meaning. But there is to be no doubt unintended implicit recipients are to be avoided at all costs. For while the former may operate to our benefit by expressing to others what they have overheard the latter will be to our detriment should they express to others what was intended for a specific recipient; that recipient being the intended implicit recipient only.

As the implied meaning of what we have expressed is our honest expression often it is very recipient specific and contains within it a meaning when shared with those who are not the intended recipient most likely will be taken as offensive. That is not to say all implicitly honest expressions are offensive expressions or all offensive expressions are implicitly honest expressions. Rather it is to say that once an expression is expressed the implied meaning may be misunderstood by unintended recipients as it may also be misunderstood by intended recipient. So it is stated by one Henry Delaune:

> *'Think all you speak; but speak not all you think: Thoughts are your own; but your words are so no more. Where Wisdom steers, wind cannot make you sink: Lips never err, when she does keep the door''*

We hate to state at this time or any time known to us in human history the intended recipient will be most likely to understand or be more understanding of a misunderstanding than the unintended who will seek to better what they perceives as an offender or inferior being. Such desire of betterment on the part of the unintended implicit recipient is commonly not for the betterment of the offender but rather for the affirmation of the virtue of the unintended recipient. More will be written on this in the Understanding section to follow.

Unlike the explicit expression which must always have a minimum of a single recipient be they intended or unintended, the self or others; an implicit expression may have two possible recipients, those being either someone or no one. The former is the intended recipient when we are being honest the latter when we are being deceitful or deceptive. The phenomenon in which the implicit recipient is everyone does occur though in such rarity it need not be examined by us here but will be commented on a little later.

For those who would question the logic behind our statement there may be no implicit recipient of an implicit expression we would point out in the event we wish to practice social deceit or self deception; that is to say deceit of another person or deception of our own person by our person to such an extent we may not discern the implicit honest expression from the deceitful or deceptive expression there is no need of an audience.

Since the implicit recipient is the being which was intended to receive the honest implicit meaning and in the case of social deceit or self-deception the audience may be represented is another or the self; should the self not disclose honestly to another or the self than we must state the implicit recipient; that is the recipient of the implicit honest meaning does not exist as either an external or internal entity.

As neither the former or the latter are to receive the honest implicit meaning. Where the former shall not receive it by means of the efforts of the self at deceit of another and the latter shall not receive it by the very nature of the deception of the self in communion with the self; thereby excluding all that is not the self in said communion. Hence there is no need of any external entity or the self when giving a dishonest implicit expression for no entity shall receive the honest implicit meaning of our implicit expression.

To state there are times when there are no implicit recipients should not come as a shock; indeed we affirm when we wish to exercise deceit or deception our own focus is more on others attaining our explicit meaning and not our implicit meaning. In the case of ethical deceit our intention is the person whom we are speaking with shall be only an explicit recipient and in no way is to receive the implicit meaning and in the case of moral deception we intend to convince ourselves of the explicit meaning and to not divulge any implicit meaning to ourselves; thereby making ourselves the explicit recipient.

So long as there is a sensical expression; that is to say an honest explicit expression there must always be an explicit recipient to receive the expression. Be that recipient one's self or something outside of the self. However we would venture so far to say it is not possible for another to be the implicit recipient without ourselves being an implicit recipient. For while we may deceive ourselves without others knowing it is not possible for us to be honest with others with out us knowing we are being honest. Thus if there is an implicit recipient that is not the self than the self is also an implicit recipient.

As such it is essential when making any expression be it deceitful, deceptive, or honest to have explicit recipients. Yet when being deceitful or deceptive it is possible to be devoid of any implicit recipients. When we wish to deceive or be deceptive we precisely intend the implicit meaning of what is being expressed is hidden from the recipient in question. If well hidden than not noticed; if unnoticed than not perceived; if unperceived than non-existent; if non-existent than non-existent as either entity (object) or as recipient (subject); if hidden than existent as entity (object); if existent as entity (object), but non-existent as perception than non-existent as recipient (subject). So it is put to us by one Hannah Arendt:

> *"The trouble with lying and deceiving is that their efficiency depends entirely upon a clear notion of the truth that the liar and deceiver wishes to hide. In this sense, truth, even if it does not prevail in public, possesses an ineradicable primacy over all falsehoods."*

The Intent of Expression

We must presently inform our readers for the sake of explanation we were differentiating the explicit expression and the implicit expression respectively as the expression which conveys either the explicit meaning or the implicit meaning. The reality is the explicit and implicit meanings are expressed in one single all encompassing expression and not two separate ones. The single encompassing expression is made up of words in accordance with an explicit expression and will have an implied meaning in accordance with an implicit expression; be that implied meaning expressed by the expresser or derived by the recipient.

Having explained the meaning of our terms we are now able to explain the means by which the intent of an expression may be determined. We previously stated it is the interaction of the aforementioned variables will lead us to three inevitable intents of expression. Those intents being a purely honest expression which we will cautiously title Truth; it is to be noted this truth is the truth of a true or explicitly and implicitly honest expression. Truth as we are expressing is not necessarily absolute truth though it may often be in accordance with absolute truth. Neither is it relative truth, though we must admit it is relative to our ability to express. It is expressive truth, which is to say it is the truest honest expression which we are capable of constructing for the absolute or relative truth which we conceive or perceive of.

We must take the time to point out expressive truth is viewed on the part of the expresser. While we must state the expresser considers the effects of the expression to be made on the recipient we do presently recognize as previously stated our understanding of others may only be rudimentary. As such there is a possibility for our expression to be misunderstood though not our intention. More shall be explained regarding this in the next section.

The True expression as we define it occurs solely when explicit and implicit variables are all equal. That is to say expressive truth occurs when the explicit and implicit meanings are the same and when the explicit and implicit recipients are the same. As expected all things must be in congruence with one another to express the truest possible statement we can. We shall endeavor to express what we have stated in another more concise manner so as to ensure what we have said is sensible based on the words of Antoine Laviodier and Clifford Truesdell:

> *"Languages are true analytical methods. Algebra, the means of expression which is the simplest, most exact and best adapted to its object, is both a language and an analytical method. In short, the art of reasoning can be reduced to a well-constructed language."*

And

> *"There is nothing that can be said by mathematical symbols and relations which cannot also be said by words. The converse, however, is false. Much that can be and is said by words cannot successfully be put into equations, because it is nonsense."*

Where we to define expressive truth as a math function we would see expressive truth occurs only when the value of the Intent of Expression IE = 0. As shown in the equation below where each variable is to be assigned a whole number value that corresponds to each meaning and each recipient. If both meanings are the same; that is to say honest or dishonest, the same number value is to be applied to both meaning variables. If the recipients are the same the same numeric value is applied to both recipient variables. Otherwise each variable is to be assigned its own distinct number values such that meaning variables do not equal recipient variable values; where the variables are defined such that M_E is the explicit meaning; M_I is implicit meaning; R_E is the explicit recipient; and R_I is the implicit recipient:

$$IE = (M_E - M_I) + (R_E - R_I) \text{ such that } M_{E,\,I} \neq R_{E,\,I}$$

Of course it must be recognize by our previous definitions the possibility of an expressive truth occurring in which the explicit and implicit meaning are not honest explicit and implicit meanings is simply not possible. This may be affirmed by our definitions of an honest explicit expression. A requirement of an expressive truth demanding explicit and implicit meaning be the same; both must either be honest or dishonest at the same time. Were the explicit meaning to be dishonest it would end up being nonsensical as we have previously defined. A nonsensical expression is considered to have no intent as it makes no sense and will most assuredly be regarded as nonsense by the explicit and/or implicit recipient.

Having determined the means by which we may measure the intent of expressions and the conditions required for the ideal honest expression it is now stated by us in the case of ethical deceit or moral deception the one variable that shall remain consistent is of the explicit meaning. By means of conceptual observation we acknowledged any form of deceit or deception is dependant on the appearance of expressive truth. As such deceit or deception must not only avoid being nonsensical but must also incorporate as much of an honest expression as possible to avoid becoming insensible.

The necessity for any useful form of deceit or deception to avoid nonsensicality and still maintain sensibility has been expressed by us earlier in the argument under the section of the Explicit Meaning of Expression for the former and the Purpose of Expressions for the latter. We maintain the necessity of avoidance of nonsensicality and inclusion of sensibility is not due to some aesthetic desire on our part as the author for a wonderful piece of literature but is due to an aesthetic requirement of the recipients of expression.

We do presently state sensicality (which is currently not a word but would be the opposite of nonsensicality or not nonsensicality) is a function of the explicit meaning of our expression. Similarly sensibility is a function of the implicit meaning of our expression. Such a statement must be made by us for in our Intent of Expressions equation all adjectives which are to be applied to meaning must be assigned to either the explicit or implicit variables for meaning. As we have previously shown sensicality is tied to our explicit variable it stands to follow sensibility is tied to our implicit variable. As the former is concerned with the externalization of meaning so the latter is concerned with the internalization of meaning.

As the world we seek to describe is the actual world which consists of honesty and dishonesty the development of skepticism in humans and to an extent in animals is inherent to the nature of survival. Skepticism calls to attention ambiguities and as we have expressed earlier ambiguity degrades confidence and promotes prudence. Thus it is the nature of all creatures to be wary of ambiguity. In the human species prudence is exercised should an expression not be aesthetically pleasing to the recipient as meaning or in action; in thought or expression. That is to say the expression will be deemed insensible even if said expression avoids being nonsensical. This is commonly referred to in engineering as a sanity check, which is a check to verify if an explanation is reasonable.

So great is the requirement of sensibility that we are hard pressed to even conceive of a situation in which our thoughts, emotions, or instincts are devoid of sensibility. As expressions may only be expressions of the aforementioned parts of our person we recognize our expressions must also be sensible especially if they are to be believable. So it is put to us by Immanuel Kant:

> *"All thought must, directly or indirectly, by way of certain characters, relate ultimately to intuitions, and therefore, with us, to sensibility, because in no other way can an object be given to us."*

We recognize in our youth our ignorance and gullibility allows for more insensible expressive falsities to be perceived as truths. Though this is the case we must still point out an utterly insensible expressive falsity will not be taken as an expressive truth even by a child. We trust we need not delve deeply into the necessity of sensibility of a falsity for it to be regarded as truth. We wish to make note that what is sensible is not only what is possible but also what is probable; where as that which avoids being nonsensical at best is sensible, which is to say possible and probable; and at worst insensible or impossible.

We trust with time our readers have heard enough falsities to determine the difference between a sensible one and an insensible one. We also trust our readers may recognize upon retrospection the falsities which were effective and which were not in convincing them they were expressive truths though they were not. As such we shall give no more examples at this moment since we are well aware life itself has equipped us with a plethora of examples to draw from in regards to this subject.

Ethical Deceit

Now we have established the one fixed variable in our Intent of Expression definition is of the explicit meaning and we should endeavor to retain as much honesty as possible so as to have our expression be believable we may continue our explanation to divulge the conditions of ethical deceit and moral deception. As it has been held by us throughout our entire work ethical is to be in terms of the external and moral in terms of the internal. From this we see any failure of an expression to be an expressive truth, that is to say it is an expressive falsity is when the Intent of Expression does not equal zero (IE $\neq$ 0) may only occur in regards to the external representation (Ethical Deceit), which we accounted for in our function as the recipients of expression or in an internal representation (Moral Deception), which is accounted for by the meaning of expressions.

Ethical Deceit occurs when the condition for IE $\neq$ 0 is due to the recipients of expression not matching; that is to say $R_E \neq R_I$. Ethical Deceit is when we intend to deceive someone else. As argued by us earlier the deceit of another is dependent on the recipient and not on the meaning. It may be argued by others based on our own writings above that ethical deceit is also caused by an inequality in the value of the explicit and implicit meanings; that is to say $M_E \neq M_I$. While this may occur during times of ethical deceit this we have determined is not the defining characteristic of ethical deceit but is the defining characteristic of moral deception.

While it is true the explicit and implicit meaning may not be congruent in ethical deceit this is only when viewed in regards to a single recipient. That is to say if expresser "A" were to be ethically deceitful to recipient "A" by means of an incongruence of meaning then what we would be forced to argue is the explicit meaning is honest (as it must be for it to avoid nonsensicality) but the implicit meaning is devoid of honesty. However we would point out to our critics that to make such an assertion while avoiding nonsensicality would cause us great difficulty in regards to maintaining sensibility.

Similarly were we forced to agree with our critics we would be forced to say that the explicit and implicit meanings do not have the same value. Upon admission of such a case we would then be hard pressed to define why it is ethical deceit is still an action worth engaging in. Needless to say we recognize quite blatantly that to express when expression is not needed is a waste of our time and to deceive when deceit is not needed is to increase the probability of being exposed as a deceiver. To avoid exposure the wise will deceive only when necessary so as to decrease the number of deceitful statements by which they maybe exposed. As such argument for the utilization of an expression to practice ethical deceit in which the explicit and implicit meanings are not both honest is foolish. For we would not express when we need not and we would not deceive when the truth will suffice; rather we will be silent when we can and will avoid introducing deceit when not necessary so as not to have our other deceits discovered. So it has been stated by one Adrienne Rich and Alexander Pope:

> *"Lying is done with words and also with silence."*

And

> *"He who tells a lie is not sensible of how great a task he undertakes; for he must be forced to invent twenty more to maintain that one."*

Thus the goal of ethical deceit is not actually to lie. Rather it is to intentionally deliver different information to various recipients.

It is fully intended by the expresser for the explicit and implicit recipients to receive an honest expression. What is not intended by the expresser is for the explicit recipient to receive the honest implicit meaning. The implicit meaning is to be only received by the implicit recipient should one be desired though the explicit meaning may be received by both the explicit and implicit recipients (argument was made for this previously.)

In regards to the explicit recipient it must be affirmed the intention of ethical deceit is to have the general consensus of explicit recipients be they one or many receive, conceive, or perceive only of the explicit meaning of what is expressed. That is not to say one does not take into consideration the implicit meaning the explicit recipient will derive from the expression. On the contrary it is to say the intent of the expresser is to have the explicit recipient derive an implicit meaning from the explicit meaning of the expression given that is not the actual implicit meaning given to the implicit recipient. Hence in terms of the implicit meaning M_I to the explicit recipient R_E and the implicit recipient R_I we must state:

R_E Derives M_I from expresser
R_I Receives M_I from expresser (should an intended R_I exists.)

(It is to be noted the phenomenon commonly referred to as a double entendre is an honest expression in which the explicit and implicit recipient is the same person and the recipient is intended to both receive the implicit meaning as well as derive the implicit meaning from the explicit expression. Thus the double entendre where the received meaning is the intended implicit meaning and the derived implicit meaning is the double meaning. As the secondary meaning is derived it tends to be more perverse than the primary meaning. This is explained later on in the section concerning Understanding.)

Earlier we stated the explicit meaning is derived from the commonality of an implicit meaning. That is to say when we sought to express a particular thing we commonly used the same expression among all the members of our society. Over time this expression became the expression to express that meaning and thus the expression acquired an explicit meaning or general meaning of the particular expression; what is often termed as the meaning of the words. This was shown above by means of an equation of explication, where $\bar{E}_E$ is the **average** explicit expression, E_E is a **particular** explicit expression, M_I is the implicit meaning, and M_E is the explicit meaning:

$$M_E = \bar{E}_E / M_I$$

It is critical one realizes in the defining of the explicit meaning it is the **average** explicit expression used and not a **particular** explicit expression. It is the utilization of a **particular** expression consistently thereby defining the **average** expression for a given implicit meaning gives rise to explicit meaning. We must insist the **average** explicit expression is the **average** expression taken in relation to the consistent **particular** explicit expressions used. Hence the consistent use of **particular** expressions allows us to specify an **average** expression used. Such is a mathematical average or mean and such is the meaning utilized here.

When implicating or deriving an implicit meaning from an explicit expression in relation to an explicit meaning we see our function becomes invalid. The invalidity of the function is caused by the explicit expression. While the explicit meaning is defined in terms of the **average** explicit expression $\bar{E}_E$ in relation to the implicit meaning M_I; the implication or derived implicit meaning utilizes the **particular** explicit expression E_E in relation the explicit meaning M_E. Use of a **particular** explicit expression is invalid for defining either the explicit or implicit meaning, as shown below:

$$M_E \neq E_E / M_I => M_I \neq E_E / M_E$$

While we recognize implication of an implicit meaning by means of a particular explicit expression in relation to the explicit meaning does not yield the actual implicit meaning we also recognize such a derivation may yield a similar implicit meaning as the actual implicit meaning the closer the particular explicit expression is to the average expression. Thus the actual implicit meaning may be approximated by derivation in the best case, commonly will not be in the normal case as the intent of ethical deceit is it will not, and may bear no relation to the actual implicit meaning in the worst case. As re-expressed below by the equations:

$$M_I \approx E_E / M_E \quad \text{(Best Case in which } E_E \approx \text{ or } = \bar{E}_E\text{)}$$
$$M_I \neq E_E / M_E \quad \text{(Normal and Worst Case)}$$

Ethical deceit makes use of this process of implication or deriving an implicit meaning, which we have stated at best yields an implicit meaning similar to the actual implicit meaning and at worst yields an entirely different implicit meaning than the actual implicit meaning. Ethical deceit intends for the explicit recipient to receive the honest explicit meaning by means of an explicit expression and from this derive an honest implicit meaning which is not in accordance with the actual honest implicit meaning of the expression. Though this derivation is not the actual implicit meaning it is not to be confused with misunderstanding as it was the intent of the expresser to have the recipient derive an implicit meaning which is not to be the actual implicit meaning.

The derived implicit meaning is also an honest implicit meaning though it is not the actual implicit meaning expressed by the expresser. As it is derived by the explicit recipient from the explicit expression and meaning it will retain sensicality, as the honest explicit expression and meaning must be sensical to be honest, and it will retain the level of sensibility required by the explicit recipient to make it believable; if and only if the explicit expression and meaning allow for the derivation of a sensible implicit meaning. Thus the wrong explicit expression and/or meaning given will not allow for a sensible derived implicit meaning and will be immediately recognize by the explicit recipient as a fallacy. So it is expressed by Carl Gustav Jung:

> *"If one does not understand a person, one tends to regard him as a fool."*

In the event a sensible implicit meaning is derivable from the sensical explicit expression and meaning the derived implicit meaning is an honest implicit meaning due to its sensibility and the explicit meaning is honest due to the sensicality of the explicit expression. We now reaffirm it is not equality of explicit and implicit meaning in our Intent of expression function that determines ethical deceit, as meaning variables are indeed equal as both the explicit and implicit meanings are honest; rather inequality in the explicit and implicit recipients of our function is the determining factor for ethical deceit. As the explicit recipient must derive an honest implicit meaning for themselves and the implicit recipient receives the actual honest implicit meaning from the expresser.

We have stated ethical deceit always requires a recipient. Previously we were only referring to the need of an explicit recipient. However what is to be recognized is there is always an implicit recipient as well! This recipient may either be an external implicit recipient or an internal implicit recipient. We state this is so due to the requirement of sensibility. This requirement is as we have shown required by the recipient. As such it is required by the expresser as well. Hence when the expresser practices ethical deceit they always endeavor to satisfy sensibility be the implicit recipient external and internal or simply internal.

Satisfaction of the expresser's sense of sensibility denotes the expresser is an implicit recipient of their own expression. As we have stated above all of this is necessary in the fulfillment of the requirement of sensibility. The requirement for sensibility is argued as a purpose of expression; for we have maintained and adhere to the reasonable assumption one does not invest effort in ethical deceit to be seen as deceitful and any expression devoid of sensibility will be viewed as deceitful by any recipient.

The intended implicit recipient must also be an explicit recipient. It is impossible for us to say an external implicit recipient would grasp any meaning without an expression of some type. Any expression will have associated with it an explicit meaning and implicit meaning for the expression must be sensical and sensible. As the recipient requires both sensicality and sensibility the recipient must receive both the explicit and implicit expressions though the recipient is categorized as either the explicit or implicit recipient. The external intended recipient is intended to receive the honest implicit meaning; as a consequence they will receive an honest explicit meaning by way of the expression which must be sensical in order to even attempt being sensible.

In the case of the external implicit recipient the need for an expression is necessary for the implicit meaning to be conveyed beyond the self. The expression must be sensical to the recipient and to the expresser. In the case of the internal implicit recipient the verification of the explicit expression for sensibility which is to be derived by the explicit recipient requires the expression to be verified for sensicality. As it is not possible for the expresser to verify the sensicality of the expression by means of the recipients senses the need arise for verification of sensicality by the self. This verification of the expression by the self causes the internal implicit recipient or the self to become an explicit recipient as well.

What must be stressed is whether the implicit recipient is internal or external when the explicit and implicit recipients are not the same person than the person or persons who are intended to be only explicit recipients are being deceived. Those recipients that are both explicit and implicit recipients are as our previous equation states receiving the true honest expression. As the explicit recipient is anyone capable of hearing the explicit expression one would state anyone overhearing a conversation is being deceived. Such is not the case due to the intent of the expresser as those overhearing a conversation are neither the intended explicit or implicit recipients. We will cover this in greater detail in the Understanding section to follow.

Understanding

In the previous section we stated our explanation would seem to state anyone overhearing our conversation is being deceived. That is to say we unintentionally practice ethical deceit as regards eavesdroppers. Needless to say we may not admit such a thing as it would be in contradiction to our assumption one is deceitful only when need be. If one were to be deceitful unintentionally than we would be admitting one is deceitful when they do not need to be or unnecessarily. Having given explanation for ethical deceit we must now discuss the act of misunderstanding to fully explain why there is no unintentional deceit in regards to eavesdroppers.

First we must state the subject of misunderstanding is being discussed at this time for one reason. That reason being misunderstanding may only occur in the ethical sense and not in the moral sense. Following the definition of ethical (external) and moral (internal) utilized throughout our entire works what we mean to say is one may be misunderstood by another, but one may never misunderstand themselves. We may stipulate this based on observation misunderstanding may only occur when the implicit meaning is conveyed.

When the implicit recipient is the self then there is no need of conveyance as the self is fully aware of what the self intends to convey. However when the implicit recipient is not the self then conveyance is required and accomplished by means of an expression. As the expression is meant to convey the implicit meaning to the external implicit recipient it would be foolish of us to state or assume this goal is accomplished every time. Indeed while it is accomplished most of the time it may not be accomplished enough times that consideration must be given to the phenomena. When it is not accomplished there is most assuredly a misunderstanding between the implicit meaning conveyed by the expresser and the implicit meaning received by the implicit recipient.

Second we must express there are two types of Misunderstanding; the first being misapprehension, which may be considered to truly be the lack of understanding and is deserving of the title misunderstanding. The second being misconstruction, which is more properly referred to as the opposite of understanding or condescension. The former is a test of our humility; our ability to be silent, to listen, and to come to understand. The latter a testament of our vanity; our tendency to speak when we should not, to degrade our fellow man, to promote our self image, and to revel in our own self assigned greatness as stated by Charles Colton, Marcus Tullius Cicero and Ezra Taft Benson.

> *""The greatest friend of truth is time, her greatest enemy is prejudice, and her constant companion humility."*

> *"Silence is one of the great arts of conversation."*

And

> *"Pride is concerned with who is right. Humility is concerned with what is right."*

Misapprehension which we will associate with improper implication is when the implicit meaning is not properly understood. We previously stated the implicit meaning is delivered to the implicit recipient for both the honest expression and during ethical deceit. Though this honest implicit meaning is provided for the implicit recipient the implication, that is to say what is implied by this implicit meaning, of this implicit meaning may not be understood as intended. Thus the improper implication of the implicit meaning is simply a misunderstanding due to misapprehension.

Improper implication may arise from a myriad of factors; however we stress the most common cause of improper implication is the very subject which we have made reference too before. That subject being the relationship between the expresser and the recipient. We have stated it is necessary the expresser have an understanding of the recipient. Indeed we hold the greater the understanding of the recipient by the expresser the less chance for misapprehension.

We must further state the relationship between the expresser and the recipient is not solely expresser to recipient. For just as the understanding of the recipient by the expresser decreases the chances of misapprehension so to does the understanding of the expresser by the recipient avoid misapprehension. It is to be noted the greater the understanding of the expresser and of the recipient the more assured the information communicated will not deviate from its intended meaning.

This relationship between expresser and recipient must exist even on a rudimentary level for any communication to exist. This mutual understanding of persons facilitates the sharing and receiving of the expresser and the recipient by promoting the most crucial trait for communication; humility. For humility gives rise to temperance, temperance gives rise to patience, patience to wisdom, and ultimately wisdom gives rise to understanding. Indeed we would be very hard press to find an example of understanding not proceeded by the humility required to be silent and listen. So it is expressed to us by Saint Augustine and Rachel Naomi Remen:

> *"Humility is the foundation of all the other virtues hence, in the soul in which this virtue does not exist there cannot be any other virtue except in mere appearance."*

> *"The most basic and powerful way to connect to another*

person is to listen. Just listen. Perhaps the most important thing we ever give each other is our attention.... A loving silence often has far more power to heal and to connect than the most well-intentioned words."

We would be foolish to think misapprehension is the only type of misunderstanding. Indeed there is one other type of misunderstanding which we must discuss. This is the misunderstanding occurring in regards to an eavesdropper. We must give explanation of this else concede unintentional ethical deceit does occur. As we have expressed before to concede unintentional ethical deceit does occur is to undermine the very purpose of deceit.

Misapprehension as we have explained above occurs due to improper implication. Improper implication is not limited to but is generally caused by a lack of understanding of the people involved in a discourse. The misapprehension may be said to be the result of a lack of humility due to individuals not taking the time to come to an understanding of the people involved. However the following misunderstanding may be said to be a true testament to our vanity when we become involved.

Misconstruction is a result of improper explication. While we are going to endeavor to explain misconstruction in terms of eavesdroppers we do readily admit our analysis will also apply to any and all people engaged in conversation simply to express and in no way to receive. We will focus on eavesdroppers first and then move on to the avid speaker/non-listener known as the verbose or condescending.

We have explained the intention for the utilization of ethical deceit is to have the explicit recipient derive an implicit meaning from the expression not in accordance with the actual implicit meaning given to the implicit recipient. As we have just explained how misapprehension of the implicit meaning may occur in regards to the implicit recipient of an honest expression we must now state misconstruction occurs in regards to unintended explicit recipients in either an honest or deceitful expression.

While we have stated previously that unintended explicit recipients are acceptable as they may be useful we were not stating they are desirable. Unlike misapprehension, which we may state is a function of the understanding of those who partake in a given discourse; misconstruction is purely a function of the unintended explicit recipient's pride, perversion, and/or piousness.

Upon entering into a conversation as an unintended explicit recipient we stress that which occurs in terms of ethical deceit for the intended explicit recipient readily occurs for the unintended explicit recipient. That is to say the unintended recipient shall derive an implicit meaning from the expression which they hear. This derived implicit meaning may be in accordance with the actual implicit meaning but commonly will be divergent.

As the expression was initial constructed by the expresser to account for the particulars of the intended explicit recipient and the recipient in question is familiar with the subject of conversation and the pretext of the discussion the derived implicit meaning by the intended explicit recipient is one which we would call a derivation of understanding given the information presented.

The unintended explicit recipient however is devoid of all of the benefits of the intended explicit recipient. The expression was not constructed with consideration of the particular of the unintended recipient and the understanding of the recipient in question to the subject and the pretext of the conversation is most assuredly lacking.

As such sufficient conditions for a properly derived implicit meaning are not present. Though sufficient conditions are not present we assure our reader an improper derivation/explication will occur based on another set of criterion. The criterion for the explication of an implicit meaning by an unintended explicit recipient will as with other things when sufficient external criterion does not persist be founded on the understanding of the self rather than on the understanding of the expresser or the situation.

That is to say the explicated implicit meaning will always be such as to provide the opportunity for moral (internal) gratification; meaning the explicated implicit meaning will always be one causing a degradation of the expresser in the perception of the unintended explicit recipient. This is what we have earlier referred to as the testament to the pride, perversion, and/or piousness of the unintended explicit recipient.

Manifestation of the pride of the unintended explicit recipient is noted in the tendency of one who has entered a conversation they were not to be part of to correct the last person to have spoken. This maybe sited as the "Prove them wrong" phenomenon of humans. Such a phenomenon as we well know satisfies our sense of superiority. A sense harbored in all humans to such an extent were we to come across a person devoid of a sense of superiority in regards to their fellow humans we state they would be deemed to have esteem issues and are unwell.

Reiteration of an expression in a perverse manner is well known to any and all persons who are or have passed through adolescence. Needless to say we recognize sexuality is dominant subject of the human creature upon the onset of adolescence and until the death of the person in question. Such interest is often times exaggerated by the forced suppression in some societies and by the openness of it in others. Nonetheless we recognize as a means for the unintended explicit recipient to prove their superiority and interject themselves into the conversation it is not uncommon to take the words of the expresser and from that derive a perverse implicit meaning. The perversion of this meaning is dependant on the situation perceived by the unintended explicit recipient.

In the case of a situation of conservatism the perversion will be such to imply promiscuity on the part of the expresser. In the case of a liberal situation the perversion may be such as to imply prudishness on the part of the expresser. Be the perverted explicated implicit meaning one of promiscuity or prudishness it will assuredly be such that the unintended explicit recipient shall promote their superiority over the previous expresser so as to degrade them by a sense of embarrassment or shame for lacking in what is deemed more valuable in the given situation.

The interjection of ones self into a conversation that was not intended for the self cannot be deemed as anything more then an utter testament of ones piousness. For the interjection of the self into any conversation in which the self was not an intended participator regardless of the justification for doing so is to be recognized as the pious view of the importance of the self. To interject into a conversation for any reason is to hold what is to be interjected is of more importance than what is being discussed. In the event the interjection is of the same subject matter as the conversation again it is held what shall be stated is of such importance the conversation would suffer greatly without it.

Of course we acknowledge there are indeed times where the piousness of the interjector is well warranted. For example should the lives of the conversers be in immediate jeopardy unbeknownst to them. In such a case interjection could save the lives of the conversers and is highly justified. Nonetheless it must be stressed the assumption is what is to be expressed is of more importance than the conversation occurring and is thus a testament to the piousness of the interjector; for piousness does not hinge upon justification or the lack thereof.

While we do account for the extreme case above we similarly recognize such is not the common case. Commonly we observe the interruption of a conversation is at best remotely justified and is indeed a true testament to the piousness of the interrupter. To interrupt in regards to the same subject is due to impertinence. To interrupt in regards to another subject is due to impatience.

So it may be said for either the eavesdropper or the verbose. As stated by John Locke:

> *"There cannot be greater rudeness than to interrupt another in the current of his discourse."*

We may observe all which we have stated for the eavesdropper is indeed accurate in regards to the verbose. For the goal of the eavesdropper and the verbose are the same in regards to the conversation at hand. Both wish to take the opportunity to interject their views without consideration of the views of the other people involved in the conversation. There can be no doubt what is to be interjected be it a prideful, perverted, or pious interjection shall be condescending to one or both parties engaged in the conversation. Generally the interjection is most condescending to the person who finished speaking just before the interjection. Though we wish to say people interject with praise of the last speaker it is simply a more observable situation that people interject with ridicule of the last speaker more often than praise.

Effectiveness of Deceit and Deception

Having discussed the subject of understanding we shall now complete our discourse concerning ethical deceit by explaining the means by which it is effective. It is the commonly held and justly so that part of the effectiveness of ethical deceit is tied to the gullibility of the explicit recipient. This may not be denied as the level of gullibility may be said to be proportional to the level of sensibility an expression must posses. So it is stated by Charles Darwin:

> *"Ignorance more frequently begets confidence than does knowledge. It is those who know little, and not those who know much, who so positively assert that this or that problem will never be solved by science."*

It is to be noted gullibility is also directly proportional to ignorance. The more ignorant a person is in any given subject or subjects pertaining to the given subject the more apt they are to accept insensible expressions regarding the subject as sensible. While this is a particular example it may be stated as part of a more universal reason why ethical deceit is effective.

The effectiveness of ethical deceit is summed up in one subject; trust. Generally people believe they have a good understanding of what it is to trust as they have those who they trust and those who trust in them. As with many other things it is the common held belief if one makes use of a thing they have an understanding of a thing. Often this is far from the truth of the matter for many know how to use items without knowing how those item work.

Trust is often expressed as occurring in three cases those being the innocent (*fides per insons insontis*), the necessary (*fides per necesse*), and the familiar (*fides de vulgaris*). The innocent is often used to describe family love as exists between offspring and sire. Trust of the necessary is when trust must be given in regards to an action which one cannot perform alone. Finally the familiar is characterized in terms of mates or friends. This is simply the trust we have with those who we interact with often either intimately or platonically.

All such cases are misrepresented as trust for trust is not present in any of them. We do observe people commonly wish to say one may trust without choosing (*fides per ignarus*), must trust when they are unable (*fides per incassum*), and trust what is known (*fides de notus*). While such is the case we do point out the former case is plagued with ignorance, the middle case with inability, and the latter case with confidence. All of which deplete the majesty of that which we call trust.

The innocent may not trust as they have no understanding of trust. Indeed trust is not something which may be taken upon ignorantly. Trust must be a choice on behalf of the trustee in regards to the trusted. To deprive the trustee the understanding of trust is to deprive trust of its meaning. The instilment of trust in another is an affirmation of the trustee to the trusted. Ignorant trust is simply indifference on behalf of the trustee who has no concern if the other maybe trusted.

In regards to ethical deceit the innocent are the gullible or ignorant. They are not aware deceit exists they take everything prima facie (at face value) and assume it to be honest. This assumption of honesty as opposed to an assumption of deceit is explained in our Purpose of Expression section listed above. It may not be said the innocent trust rather it may be said the innocent do not know of trust and by extension deceit; so it is ethical deceit is effective when utilized upon them for it is unexpected by them. So it is expressed by one John Updike:

> *"It is not difficult to deceive the first time, for the deceived possesses no antibodies; unvaccinated by suspicion, she overlooks lateness, accepts absurd excuses, permits the flimsiest patching to repair great rents in quotidian."*

Necessary trust is far from trust for the same reason as innocent trust. In the case of the necessary the trustee does not choose to trust so there is no trustee and trusted. Rather there is the inept and the able. The inept must acquiesce in order to continue on with their existence. The able must provide aid for it is not long before the able will be the inept as regards another situation and shall be dependent upon the ability of another.

Due to the necessity of the necessary ethical deceit is effective as regards the necessary because things must be taken prima facie (at face value). It may be said of the necessary unlike the innocent though doubt may persist, due to necessity the doubt in question must and shall be ignored. The necessary, being in a position of necessity cannot act upon the doubt as to do so may impede the pending action which is critical to the necessary. Thus ethical deceit is effective as regards the necessary for they are in no position to act upon any doubts and by their situation must accept as honest anything which is expressed.

Finally there is the so called trust of the familiar. It is within this category that ethical deceit has its true application. In the cases of the innocent and the necessary ethical deceit had the benefit of ignorance and necessity to aid in its effectiveness; we may even go so far as to say deceit was not intended for use against the innocent and the necessary as nothing said to either need be portrayed as honest since no matter what is expressed will be perceived as honest by the former due to their ignorance of dishonesty and must be accepted as honest by the latter due to their situation of necessity. However the susceptibility to deceit in regards to the innocent and the necessary is so great as to demand its usage even though it is not necessary.

In the case of the familiar ethical deceit is not without a means by which its goal is accomplished. Trust of the familiar is better termed confidence of knowledge. It is from this confidence of knowledge ethical deceit gains its effectiveness as regards the familiar. One thing must be said about all those who we claim to trust or claim to trust us that fall into the category of the familiar. That is we as they would also claim to know those we trust. Often we express this familiarity or knowledge of the trusted by the trustee is the very reason why we trust them. So it is stated by Marcus Tullius Cicero:

> *"Confidence is that feeling by which the mind embarks in great and honorable courses with a sure hope and trust in itself."*

So it is we do not trust them but rather we have confidence in our knowledge of them. By means of our confidence of knowledge we hold we may predict the action of another to such a degree we need not worry that what they do is not what we expect. By means of our confidence we establish rules unknown to the trusted they must abide by. So long as the trusted act within the rules constructed they are deemed trustworthy. Should the trusted behave in a manner contrary to the rules constructed they will often be termed erratic and untrustworthy.

Our confidence in knowledge does not only extend to the trusted but also takes into account the trustee. The treacherous acts which we ourselves have committed or recognize we can commit without remorse taint the very rules we construct for others. Such is the reason why a thief sees a world of thieves, a cheater a world of cheaters, and a liar a world of liars. It is not possible (or nearly impossible) for the rules constructed by the thief, the cheater, or the liar to see the decent as anything much more decent than themselves. The indecent in full knowledge of the treacherous acts they have committed and are capable of doing project their self upon the decent who have no interest in being indecent. So it is summed up by one Inge A. Quinn and one Henry Louise Mencken:

> *"We mistrust, for we ourselves know of the treachery we are capable of."*

And

> *"It is hard to believe that a man is telling the truth when you know that you would lie if you were in his place."*

Many of us would claim we do no such thing and genuinely trust so let us consider two examples. The first example shall be of faith which many express to be the ultimate form of trust devoid of knowledge. As it regards deities particularly those of whom there are writings which seem to express some of the actions, inclinations, or wants of said deities. It is common among many (if not all) to utilize the knowledge of these writings to impose upon said deities restrictions. Indeed to take upon themselves sovereignty of the deities by means of rules they discern from said writings in regards to the deity in question. It may commonly be observed people make statements such as, "God/s would not do that." Or "It is the will of God/s."

In such cases the faithful shall always deny they presume to dictate to the deity what the deity shall do. While they may make denial explicitly few if any will be able to avoid implicating the deity they have "faith" in must abide by certain rules. It must be stated what the faithful desire are rules the deity must follow, whether those rules are self imposed by the deity or imposed by some externality is of little or no consequence to the faith of the faithful (though such a matter will be of contestation to the theological). The rules remove ambiguity of the deity and increase confidence in said deity due to our knowledge of said rules. The rules in question must be understandable to us. For the deity to abide by rules we cannot conceive or perceive of shall not increase our knowledge and thus shall not increase our confidence in said deity. As expressed by Bridget Willard and William Ellery

Channing:

> *"We get so focused on micromanaging God and His Kingdom that we forget to realize that He is more than capable of handling things on his own!"*

And

> *"Our leading principle in interpreting Scripture is this, that the Bible is a book written for men, in the language of men, and that its meaning is to be sought in the same manner as that of other books. We believe that God, when he speaks to the human race, conforms, if we may so say, to the established rules of speaking and writing. How else would the Scriptures avail us more, than if communicated in an unknown tongue?"*

The second example shall be of a cheating mate. Such a thing is consider a great betrayal of trust by all. In the cases of discovered infidelity the common statement made by the cheated in regards to the cheater is, "I thought I knew them. I never thought they would do something like this." This very statement denotes two things which we have said before. First the cheated or trustee imposes a definition upon the cheater or another to eliminate the ambiguity/uncertainty of the other. Second upon the belief of the self that a sufficient level of ambiguity has been eliminated or a sufficient level of knowledge about the other has been obtained to have confidence in ones predictions of the actions of the other is the moment when "familiar trust" or more precisely confidence of knowledge is established.

The trust of the familiar as with the explicit meaning of words and expressions is dependent upon the utilization over time. By observation over time the trustee may determine a modality to the actions of those who are being considered for trust. It must be stressed this modality of actions shall be skewed to some degree or another based on the treachery the trustee has committed in their life time. The value of the treachery is not simply determined as a matter of quantity but is to be considered as a value of quality compounded by quantity. The closer the potential trusted acts are in accordance to the modality of action determined by the trustee the more trusted the individual becomes. So it is we seek not to acknowledge the individuality of one another but to mechanize the actions of our fellow humans by some modal rule which they must adhere to; hence trust of the familiar may be expressed in a similar mathematical manner to that of explicit meaning:

$$FT = {}_a\int^b (A/A_M)/(T(b-a))dA = \bar{A}/(A_M T)$$

Where FT is familiar trust, A is the action taken by the individual in any particular situation, A_M is the modality of actions establish by the trustee for the individual (or the rules establish by the trustee which the trusted are to follow to be trusted), T is the level of treachery committed by the trustee such that $1 \leq T < \infty$ where 1 is for a person who has committed no treachery and ∞ is for a person who commits nothing but treachery, and $\bar{A}$ is the average actions of the individual over time. From the equation we observe the closer the actions of a potential trusted coincide with the modality of actions established by the trustee the more trusted the trusted becomes by the trustee. It is to be noted the rules which make up the modality of actions often are not explicitly known to the trustee who constructed the rules. Though we say this we do stress the implication of the rules are very well known; the conclusions of the rule are also known (especially when the action is not in accordance with the conclusion of the rule). While the explicit rule is not known the implicit sense of violation from breaking the rules will be of great consideration to the trustee and most egregious.

(Math Note: It has been asked why the integration is taken as continuous and not as discreet. Explanation for this is summed up in the constant vigilance of the trusted by the trustee. There are no specific (discreet) actions which determine if the trusted is trustworthy to the trustee. Rather the trustee formulates their evaluation based on any and all phenomenon they observe of the trusted through out the duration of observation, which is without limit (continuous). When questioned if one trusts the trusted the continuous shall be integrated in the manner expressed above to create a discreet evaluation by means of the average actions of the individual in regards to the modality of actions determined for the individual by the trusted. The closer this ratio approaches the value of one the more the trusted is trusted by the trustee.)

While one good deed does not redeem a man from a life time of bad deeds, one bad deed is enough to condemn a man for a life time regardless of all his good deeds. With all averages we admit there is a possibility one value may be so far off as to permanently skew the data. Such is the case with mathematical averages and such is the case with the evaluation of trustworthiness by the trustee. The ability of a single data point to skew the data for the duration of the study period is an example of a single bad action forever instilling mistrust in that person in the eyes of the trustee. The bad action or mistrustful action may be of such consequence and be so damaging to the FT ratio that observation/knowing of the individual in question may be ceased by the trustee. In such a case we acknowledge the discreet act was of such consequence as to demand a trust evaluation at the present moment without allowing sufficient time to offset said act with other more benevolent actions. It is likely the snap evaluation shall end in a decision of untrustworthiness by the trustee in regards to the trusted.

Due to this snap evaluation of trust caused by an unworthy act we observe the subject of trust may be termed relative and the subject of mistrust absolute. For trust must be continuously earned and relates every action taken to the modality of actions established by the trustee over an unending evaluation period. Once an untrustworthy action has taken place the evaluation period ceases and sufficient time is not provided to allow the act to be remedied. Indeed should the offender seek to remedy the act no matter the means there shall always remain a doubt of the trustee due to the mistrust the act affected. So we observe the former is termed as relative for it is in full duration and relation to the modality of actions; the latter is absolute for no actions shall absolve its occurrence, so stated by Publilius Syrus:

> *"Confidence, like the soul, never returns when it has once departed"*

It would be our greatest joy for our explanation to be the perfect articulation of the root cause for one indiscretion to offset a life time of virtue. However our explanation makes a glaring over-simplification for the sake of numerical explanation. The over-simplification is we hold the value of previous acts as constant when evaluated due to an indiscretion. Such an assumption is made for simplification purposes but it must and need be recognized the known indiscretion of a given individual is more likely to be an indiscretion they commit commonly as opposed to the most severe indiscretion they have committed which would occur very rarely. Bearing in mind we fully recognize our explanation gives the individual the benefit of the doubt in regard to past actions and does not adjust for the previously unperceived maliciousness of those particular actions. Such is perfectly articulated by one Inge A. Quinn:

> *"One bad deed is enough to condemn someone for a life-time. The bad you are aware of is not the worst done. It is the most common."*

We do confess the process we outline is the mechanical process by which trust of the familiar is established. While this is the case we make no denial the values of A, Ā, A_M, T, and the study/observation period are entirely subject to the determinations of the trustee. While the values of the variables are determined subjectively by the trustee is not to say there is no means of manipulation by the trusted. Since the determination of trust by the trustee is dependent on the continuous observation of the trusted the evaluation of trust may be skewed by simply ensuring ones actions/appearance is that which they know the trustee seeks to find. Utilizing the bias of the trustee allows one who is not what the trustee would deem trustworthy to be considered such due to either insufficient observational period or improper evaluation of actions both of which are due to personal bias of the trustee. So it is stated by one Niccolo Machiavelli:

> *"Men in general judge more by the sense of sight than by the sense of touch, because everyone can see, but only a few can test by feeling. Everyone sees what you seem to be, few know what you really are, and those few do not dare take a stand against the general opinion."*

As with the deities above and our fellow man below it is the nature of man to mechanize all he perceives in order to have confidence in what he may know. Such is explained by us in our chapter concerning Ethical Categorization and Moral Definition. We observe the effort to remove ambiguity to an acceptable level of confidence is termed trust was explained by us in regards to words, meanings, and expressions in the section titled Explicit Meaning of Expression. As expected we find the mechanism by which ethical deceit operates is the mechanism by which it is effective. So it is ethical deceit (and moral deception for that matter) is effective due to self bias or a self imposed inclination of who, what, or how another will act.

Such bias may be manifested in a mathematical example where one knows $1+2=3$. As this information is common to the foundation of the understanding of mathematics it is thoroughly understood by nearly every person. Thus if we posit the question of $1+x=3$ and ask for the solution we shall determine either by algebraic methods or by association to what is known that $x=2$. However this determination is a prime example of our self bias. For what we determine is the value of x has the principal effect of

2 but may not necessarily take the form of 2. Thus x could take the form of 8/4, ((-2)^2)/2, 6/3, or any combination of digits having the principal effect of 2 when substituted for x.

While we ourselves have stated anything which is the same in all but principal is principally the same such a statement is invalid when it comes to the subject of deceit and deception which is particularly concerned with the correlation of the principal function to the form. As mathematics endeavors to determine the principal function and neglects the form; similarly the process of implication endeavors to determine the principal function while neglecting the form. Within both mathematics and implication it is commonly assumed the principal function denotes the true form. Such is the ideal case mathematically and expressively, but the subject of deceit and deception specifically seeks to utilize the desire for the ideal to conceal the real. Thus deceit and deception may be observed in the following format:

True form or intended implicit meaning => x = 6/3 (will always be zero for moral deception)
Explicit expression => 1 + x = 3
Average Explicit Expression => 1 + 2 = 3
Principal function derived or implicated implicit meaning mistaken as true form => x = 2

As may be seen above the principal function of 2 is the sensical and sensible solution to the explicit expression of 1 + x = 3. However the intended implicit meaning takes the form of 6/3 not of 2. The implicated implicit meaning takes the form of 2. Since both have the principal function of solving the explicit expression both are sensible and sensical. However one is the true solution and one is the derived honest solution. While each is the same in principal they differ in form and thus one conveys one meaning, the other a different meaning. The union of principal function with the form intended is the true meaning. The derivation of the principal function from the explicit expression take as the form intended is an honest solution but not the true meaning. So it is ethical deceit and moral deception utilize the self bias of the ideal to hide the real. So it is stated by Gerog Christoph Lchtenberg:

> *"The most dangerous untruths are truths moderately distorted."*

Moral Deception

Having explained the process and effectiveness of ethical deceit we now shall give explanation to moral deception. As we have just stated moral deception similar to ethical deceit gains its effectiveness due to an individuals self bias. In regards to ethical deceit said bias is commonly created by the recipient's knowledge of the external. Similarly the bias of moral deception is created by the recipient's knowledge of the internal. While both biases are based on knowledge of their respective dominions the biases are not similar as the former bias wishes to affirm the knowledge of the external the recipient has; the latter bias is in opposition to the internal knowledge of what the recipient is or has as stated by Demosthenes.

> *"Nothing is so easy as to deceive one's self; for what we wish, that we readily believe; but such expectations are often inconsistent with the real state of things."*

In regards to ethical deceit the deceitful wish to utilize the bias of the explicit recipient to hide the implicit meaning of their statement by having the explicit recipient derive an implicit meaning from the explicit expression used. In this case it is the self bias of the external explicit recipient which seeks to affirm the knowledge of the recipient that is utilized for deceit and provides the effectiveness of the act of ethical deceit. With moral deception the bias of the internal explicit recipient is utilized to hide the implicit meaning from the self and to convince the self by means of the explicit expression of something which the self knows to not be. In both cases the self bias is of the recipient of expression. In the case of the ethical the recipient is external in the case of the moral the recipient is the internal or the self. While the location of the recipients is not physically similar the recipients in question may both be categorized as the explicit recipients.

In our section titled The Implicit Recipient of Expression we give explanation in regards to the presence or lack thereof of an implicit recipient. It is to be reaffirmed there may be no implicit recipient in either ethical deceit or moral deception. In the case of the former the incongruence between the explicit recipient and the implicit recipient is the means by which we define ethical deceit. This is due to the possibility of their being an explicit and implicit recipient while ethical deceit still occurs. However in regards to the latter case of moral deception the incongruence of recipients cannot be the means by which we define moral deception.

Moral deception must be defined as a result of the explicit and implicit meanings not being equal ($M_E \square M_I$). Such must be the definition in regards to moral deception because in the event there is an implicit recipient that recipient must and will be the same as the explicit recipient, that being an internal recipient or the self. The subject of moral deception is referring to the self in communion with the self and not with an external. Hence all recipients must be defined in terms of the self and may not be expressed in terms of another without the self. That is to say the explicit recipient must be the self and the implicit recipient may only be the self or no one.

We remind the reader an external expression must always have an explicit recipient, which may either be another and/or the self. An external expression may either have someone or no one as the implicit recipient; where someone is either another and/or the self. Similarly an internal expression must always have an explicit recipient, which is the self. An internal expression must also have the same possible implicit recipients as before; those being someone or no one; where someone may only be the self. Obeying the same rules in regards to recipients where the distinction between the external expression and the internal expression is the presence or lack thereof of an external recipient of either the explicit or implicit. The former mode of expression being intended for external communication always has an external explicit recipient and may have an external implicit recipient. The latter dealing with internal communication does not have an external recipient but will always have an internal explicit recipient and may have an internal implicit recipient.

May we find we have an internal explicit recipient without an internal implicit recipient might we call this moral deception? By our own definition we may not. To make explanation of this requires us to keep in mind the expresser and the recipient in regards to moral deception. We must remember the expresser and the recipient is one and the same when discussing moral/internal expressions. As such it is impossible for us to have an implicit meaning from the expresser not received by an implicit recipient in regards to internal expression as expresser and recipient are the same; to say otherwise is to say there is misapprehension of the self by the self.

To make such argument is of the utmost futility. We may argue misapprehension of that which is interpersonal by our person is possible due to the origin and reception not being the same. Hence the implicit meaning is not received properly by the external implicit recipient. To presume to argue we misapprehend that which is intrapersonal, originating from our person and received by our person is to say the implicit meaning which we ourselves made is unknown to us whom made it. We do confess it is possible to not be able to state explicitly that which we know implicitly but we may not nor shall we ever admit it is possible for us not to know implicitly that which is implicated by the self. Otherwise we must admit an utter contradiction where we do not understand what our understanding has created or we do not know what we know.

For clarification we are stating is that which is created by our understanding apriori is always understood apriori. That which we know aposteriori is always known aposteriori. We are not saying that which is created by our understanding apriori is always understood aposteriori or that which is know by experience aposteriori is always known apriori. If the self is the progenitor of the thought (apriori) then the thought will make sense to the self (apriori). Should one endeavor to understand the thought (apriori) based on externalities (aposteriori) or convey the thought outside the self (aposteriori) then there is no such maxim of understanding as with that which is from or by the self to the self. The case becomes either that which is from another (aposteriori) to the self (apriori) when trying to understand the thought by externalities or from the self (apriori) to another (aposteriori) when trying to share the thought with another. If one has an experience (aposteriori) which they use to form a concept (apriori) or utilize the event as an explanation of a concept (apriori) to endeavor to perform such actions becomes either an effort to generate a concept (apriori) from the conceptualization of an experience (aposteriori) or an effort to utilize experience (aposteriori) to explain a concept by a synthesis of understanding (apriori). We may stress only what arises from our understanding is understood by the self and what we know is known to the self. Apriori to apriori, aposteriori to aposteriori; any other combination is subject to misunderstanding or misapprehension.

From this we may state in regards to the moral/internal expression, if there is an implicit meaning than there is an implicit recipient. If there is no implicit recipient it is because there is no implicit meaning. So it is with internal expressions the implicit recipient is dependent upon there being an implicit meaning. To say otherwise as we have expressed is to state a contradiction of that which is created by the self and acknowledged by the self. It is to be noted we are not stating one is aware of the data within their mind to construct a thought. Rather we are stating any thought constructed shall be known to the thinker that has thought of it. We would be greatly mistaken in establishing the criterion of moral deception as that of incongruence of recipients as we have previously done with ethical deceit. Due to the inability of the self to hide what is derived by the self from the self we find our definition is far more accurate in the case of moral deception if we define it in terms of an incongruence of meaning since the presence of implicit meaning or lack thereof determines if there is an implicit recipient or not.

The question then becomes what is the process of moral deception? Since our person is unable to hide from our person that which is derived by our person than deception of the self should be utterly impossible. While we may make such a statement we may not deny the ability of an individual to perform self deception. Such a statement would not express the reality though for many it expresses their individual, inhuman ideology. Unbeknownst to our reader we have already laid out and explained in great detail the means and method of moral deception. We take this moment to express to the reader the unity of our explanation by stating that which they have just read regarding ethical deceit is the same explanation for moral deception.

While the subjects of ethical deceit and moral deception are not the same thing the process by which they work is exceedingly similar. Indeed should the reader only take into account the following difference they shall find the explanation for ethical deceit is ideal for moral deception. The difference the reader needs to keep in mind is the location of the intended recipients of the explicit and implicit if there are any. For the ethical the intended recipients are external for the moral they are internal. The consideration of this fact leads us through our previous statements concerning the internal implicit recipient; the proper definition of moral deception as a difference in explicit and implicit meaning; and finally in terms moral deception the implicit meaning M_I is derived from the internal explicit expression received by R_E as an actual M_I and by extension R_I does not exist:

M_I is derived from the internal explicit expression with meaning M_E conveyed to R_E.

R_I does not exist as M_I does not exist.

The uniformity of our explanation is such that what has been previously expressed by us in the section concerning ethical deceit regarding the processes of explication and implication remains valid for the subject of moral deception with little or no augmentation required. So as to recount for our reader at this present moment we remind them the process of explication has and may be summarized in the following equation below where M_E is the explicit meaning, $\bar{E}_E$ is the average explicit expression (which in the case of moral deception is the average internal explicit expression), and M_I is the implicit meaning:

$$M_E = \bar{E}_E / M_I$$

It would seem we have an apparent flaw, as we have previously said in regards to moral deception there is no actual implicit meaning ($M_I = 0$), thus our explanation for explication appears invalid due to the value of M_I being zero leading to an unknown value for the explicit meaning. Our expression for explication yields infinite explicit meanings ($M_E = \infty$) for the average explicit expression when there is no implicit meaning. We maintain the assertion there is no implicit meaning in moral deception and point out the implicit meaning expressed in the equation for explication is not the internal implicit meaning presently nonexistent in moral deception. Rather the implicit meaning used to establish the explicit meaning by means of explication is the implicit meaning intended during honest expression as the explicit meaning to be utilized is going to be the agreed upon meaning we discussed in the beginning of our work.

The nonexistence of an actual implicit meaning in regards to moral deception does not denote the nonexistence of any implicit meaning. Internally an implicit meaning may be derived by the same process of implication which was defined for ethical deceit where the explicit meaning M_E is defined in terms of the average explicit expression $\bar{E}_E$ in relation to the universal implicit meaning M_I. The implication or derived implicit meaning M_I utilizes the particular explicit expression E_E in relation to the explicit meaning M_E. We must emphasize again that use of a particular explicit expression is invalid for defining either the explicit or implicit meaning, as shown below:

$$M_E \neq E_E / M_I => M_I \neq E_E / M_E$$

Just as with ethical deceit the implication of an implicit meaning by means of a particular explicit expression in relation to the explicit meaning does not yield the actual implicit meaning (there is no actual implicit meaning in regards to moral deception). Such implication at best may yield only a similar implicit meaning to one would have been intended had the expression been honest and not deceptive. Thus the implicit meaning created by implication shall be sensical and sensible. The implicated implicit meaning shall approach the honest implicit meaning as the explicit expression approaches the average explicit expression. It is to be noted however though the implicated implicit meaning approaches the honest implicit meaning such a phenomenon shall only increase the sensicality and sensibility of the implicated implicit meaning as there is no actual implicit meaning to approach or approximate in the case of moral deception; as expressed below by the equations:

$$M_I \approx E_E / M_E \quad \text{(Best Case in which } E_E \approx \text{ or } = \bar{E}_E)$$
$$M_I \neq E_E / M_E \quad \text{(Normal and Worst Case)}$$

While the greatest threat to ethical deceit is time the greatest catalyst to moral deception is time. Where the former is revealed by the light of temporal scrutiny the latter is disguised by temporal forgetfulness. It cannot be denied the suspicion of the human creature of that which is not of the self leads to the revelation of truth given sufficient time. This same time allows acts of self to the self to pass from memory into oblivion. We take greater note of what is expressed to us from another than we do of what is expressed to us by us. Our communion with others is fleeting; our communion with our self unending; we remember what is shared with us by another for it may not be shared with us again. We do not remember what we share with ourselves for the view is we shall share it again if need be. So it is we do prime ourselves for self deception; our recollection is convinced of our self honesty and remembers our self deception as a truth, rather than the deception it truly was. As stated by Francios de la Rochfoucauld and Thomas Paine in The Age of Reason:

> *"The intention of never deceiving often exposes us to deception."*

And

> *"It is impossible to calculate the moral mischief, if I may so express it, that mental lying has produced in society. When a man has so far corrupted and prostituted the chastity of his mind as to subscribe his professional belief to things he does not believe he has prepared himself for the commission of every other crime."*

Thus our self bias prepares us for external and self corruption.

Truth

We must emphasize again honesty is not truth. The relation of honesty and truth may best be described as the relation of expressive terms of the mind to the reality of the world (adequatio intellectus et rei: *correspondence of the mind and the reality*). The former may be said to be the expression of the perception seeking to express the reality (concordia cum veritate: *in harmony with truth*). The latter may simply be termed the reality. That the perception in no way matches the reality is something which we must admit as a possibility. At the same time we must recognize if the reality is in no way similar to the perception of it then the expression of truth is an impossibility; honest expression universal totality.

Arguments concerning the reality/actuality and perception/realization are extensive throughout the subject of philosophy. Hence we ourselves do not endeavor to argue such a matter. Rather we accept that which we perceive or realize is a perception or realization of the reality or actuality of what is. We do not say our perception or realization is the sum total of all that is. Nor do we state all of our perception realizations are. We mean to say our perceptions are always in relation to reality. Either the partial or full perception of what is or is not. In both cases our perception is in relation to the truth is as our perception is in accord with what is or in contrast to what is.

We express literary truth, mathematic truth, scientific truth, religious truth, and any other truth which we do not account for here contain with in them honest expressions which endeavor to express what is. Truth is not the transition of the honest expression to reality. Truth is reality! Not the perception of what is real but what is actually real whether perceived or not. Truth is the destination where all honest expressions intend to arrive. We do hold the correspondence theory of truth which is purported by Plato, Aristotle, and Thomas Aquinas. Though it is refuted by Immanuel Kant for the following reason:

> *"Truth is said to consist in the agreement of knowledge with the object. According to this mere verbal definition, then, my knowledge, in order to be true, must agree with the object. Now, I can only compare the object with my knowledge by this means, namely, by taking knowledge of it. My knowledge, then, is to be verified by itself, which is far from being sufficient for truth. For as the object is external to me, and the knowledge is in me, I can only judge whether my knowledge of the object agrees with my knowledge of the object. Such a circle in explanation was called by the ancients Diallelos. And the logicians were accused of this fallacy by the sceptics, who remarked that this account of truth was as if a man before a judicial tribunal should make a statement, and appeal in support of it to a witness whom no one knows, but who defends his own credibility by saying that the man who had called him as a witness is an honourable man."*

While it would seem Kant has refuted the correspondence theory expressed by previous philosophers we must point out the principal held by antiquity is not being expressed properly so as to circumvent the critique given it by Kant. For there exist within the correspondence theory and Kant's critique a glaring misnomer which appears to have permeated throughout modern philosophy. We intend to clarify here by considering the case of the liar's paradox which states, "This statement is false." The present question concerning this paradox is the relationship of the statement (explicit meaning) to the meaning of the statement (implicit meaning).

Should the explicit meaning be of the implicit meaning (assuming the recipients are the same) then the statement may be said to be expressively honest. Should the explicit and implicit meaning differ than the statement may properly be termed expressively dishonest by means of deception. As of yet we have not mentioned anything concerning the truth or falsity of the phrase only the honesty or dishonesty of the phrase. Honesty may of course be used to express truly (veritas verus: *honestly true* such as literal or analytical), honesty may also be used to hide truth (veritas falsus: *honestly false* as with plausible deniability or simple ignorance), just as dishonesty may be used to reveal truth (falsus veritas: *dishonestly true* as with theatrics, similes, metaphors, analogies, parables, sarcasm, figurative speech, etcetera), and dishonesty may be used to hide truth (falsus falsum: *dishonestly false* which is generally considered lying). The first commonly intended, the second an unintended commonality, the third commonly utilized, and the fourth a common necessity.

As the phrase in question or any phrase made in any language to articulate a liar paradox shall be sensical we observer the phrase shall always be explicitly honest. Similarly as the phrase has an implied meaning that implied meaning shall be sensible. Otherwise the statement would not be of such consideration as to be paradoxical. If it where insensible it would be consider false from the start and simply be ignored. So the liar paradox shall be implicitly honest so long as it is sensible. As we have expressed it is the overall relation of explicit to implicit meaning that determines if a phrase is honest since we are holding recipients as equal. The liar paradox consists of both sensicality (proper form) and sensibility (proper function) it can and must be termed by us as an explicitly and implicitly honest expression. Such a statement does not state an honest or dishonest intent of expression however we may state as much with proper semiotic explanation to determine the relationship between explicit and implicit meaning.

While the expression is honest in part the subject of the liar paradox is concerned with whether or not the expression is true. We hold truth is the reality and honesty is the endeavor to express reality. We already observe the parts of the expression if considered a liar paradox shall obey grammatical and semantical rules. Explanation is required to disclose the satisfaction of semantic rules which is dependent upon context (as meaning or semantics is often dependent upon the context of a phrase or expression). The liar paradox views the phrase in question devoid of context. It wishes to compare the explicit meaning with the implicit meaning of the phrase. The liar paradox also confuses honesty with truth, a simple and common misnomer causes a great deal of headache in a phrase such as the liar paradox.

First let us consider the liar paradox in context. In such a case the liar paradox does not refer to itself. Rather it would refer to a preceding or following phrase. If the preceding or following phrase is a false phrase then the statement, "this statement is false" explains the condition in a veritas verus (honestly true) manner as the phrase truly is false and such was said so. The explicit meaning and implicit meaning of the phrase was to point out the falseness of the preceding or following phrase. When the previous or following phrase is not false then we must consider the intention (by means of the context) of the phrase. As such we must consider whether the expresser is simply mistaken about the falsity of the statement and is thus speaking veritas falsus (honestly false). If so than what is said is not true and is mistaken as such by the expresser. Upon further consideration the speaker most undoubtedly would change what they have said as it is the intention of one speaking veritas falsus (honestly false) to speak veritas verus (honestly true).

Should the speaker intends sarcasm then the phrase is spoken falsus vertias (dishonestly true) as the point of saying the phrase was false was to show it is not false. In such a case the phrase is true as the intention of the expresser is to explain the reality of the phrase by means of sarcasm. While it is not likely one would speak falsus falsum (dishonestly false) with a statement such as the liar paradox we shall account for speaking in such a manner here. Should the previous or following phrase be true while the expresser knowingly states it is false when it is not then they are expressing falsus falsum (dishonestly false). There intention is to deceit or deception by mean of improper implication as we have specified earlier. It is to be noted of course the expression they will use for falsus falsum shall be sensical and sensible. As such it shall be explicitly and implicitly honest as we have defined earlier. Though we may state the expression is explicitly and implicitly honest we do not state the intent of expression is honest or the statement is true; as the intent of the expression is to not to express the reality.

In the four contextual cases we have shown above we would state the liar paradox is true. For it honestly expresses what is (veritas verus), honestly intends to express what is (veritas falsus), dishonestly expresses what is (falsus veritas), or dishonestly expresses what is not (falsus falsum). In the primary and tertiary examples the liar paradox is simply true. For both cases express the reality of the situation; one honestly the other dishonestly. In the secondary and quaternary cases the liar paradox is truly false. Each expresses that which is not true and thus may be recognized as truly not expressing the truth. As with the primary and tertiary examples the secondary and quaternary examples truly express falsely honestly and dishonestly. So it is in context the liar paradox is not paradoxically true and false simultaneously.

What of the liar paradox out of context when it refers to itself and not another? Out of context we must point out there is the intended implicit meaning of the liar paradox and the derived implicit meaning of the liar paradox. The intended implicit meaning is the true meaning of the liar paradox where as the derived implicit meaning is the meaning implicated from the explicit meaning. So long as the explicit meaning matches the intended implicit meaning then there is no need for a derived/implicated implicit meaning and the liar paradox is true without being false. Devoid of context we must simply ask the question, "What is the intent of making such a statement?" In this manner we determine the intended implicit meaning of the liar paradox. We are answered by the purpose of the liar paradox which is to exhibit to humanity a statement which adheres to grammatical and semantical rules when taken out of context appears paradoxically true and false at the same time. Next we must ask the question, "Does the statement achieve its intent?" So as to determine the explicit meaning of the statement, that is to say to determine if we need to derive/implicate an implicit meaning of the statement.

If the statement achieves its intent then the explicit meaning of the statement is in accordance with the implicit meaning of the statement; a condition which we have previously stated as a true condition in which the expression expresses the reality. Thus the liar paradox when taken out of context becomes not simply an honestly true statement (veritas verus) but rather a statement which is nothing shy of perfectly true (perfectus verus). For the statement out of context is taken as complete without any other sentences required, it is an excellent paradoxical example the likes of which there is no better, and it attains its intended purpose. If it does not achieve its purpose then the explicit meaning is not in accord with the implicit meaning. Thus the statement becomes moral deception due to the intent of expression being dishonest as determine by the statements incongruence of explicit and implicit meaning.

Great care has been taken to determine if intent of expression is intended to be honest or dishonest. Context discloses if an expression is intended to be true or false. Reality determines if truth or falsity is achieved. Such is and must be the case. For as Kant himself would recognize it is only by means of a maxum that a particum has application and meaning. The truth, which is reality, is the maxum. The honest expression of reality to another or the self is the particum. The truth of knowledge is not determined by the knowledge of truth. One may know the truth but not consider it to be true. The truth of knowledge is by its honest approximation to reality, which unknowingly or knowingly approximates or varies from truth by means of honest and dishonest expressions made to another or to the self. Knowledge of truth cannot be known devoid of expression; as cognition, realization, imagination, and revelation are all known by means of expressions. Expressions which may surmise truth in its entirety though more likely imply truth honestly or dishonestly.

Honesty

What of the subject of honesty? Indeed we have devoted an entire chapter to the subject of dishonesty. We have determined honesty by means of sensicality in grammatical form and have determined honesty by means of sensibility in its semantical form. The honesty we refer to now is not the honesty of the part but the honesty of the whole which we have gone so far as to state is the very purpose of expression. It now falls upon us to describe not only why honesty is an ethical (ab extra) and moral (ab intra) imperative but why it is forsaken by humanity when dishonesty is utilized. How is it deception takes hold even within our internal self? Such things must and should be disclosed to culminate all we have written.

To understand why we should be honest we must first understand why we become dishonest in the first place. It has been expounded by many that dishonesty is human nature. This stipulation is nothing more than a veiled attempt to maintain individualistic virtue. To state dishonesty is the nature of humanity is indirectly states the age old adage, "The Devil made me do it" to absolve humanity of responsibility for its own development. Should we consider the human creature in non-secular terms we observe humanity was not made corrupt at its inception and dishonesty is not our nature. For no religious/spiritual creationist story advocates humanity as a vile corrupt creature. Considering humanity in secular terms it is easily observed honesty is the nature of humanity as such is the tendency of humans who have first learned to speak, that is to say children.

Observation of young children who speak shows us the true nature of the human creature to honesty. Indeed so great is the honesty of children that such honesty is not acceptable to the rest of humanity as a whole and is considered offensive. Such offensiveness without a doubt is attributed to the destruction of the aforementioned self bias which is human nature. It is in order to curb this offensiveness of honesty that dishonesty is introduced to children by none other than their own parents and society in general. Dishonesty is conditioned within as right and good; we do paint this dishonesty with the fanciful title of civility and convince ourselves of it's virtue in the name of the greater good. So it is dishonesty arises not for our own sake but for the sake of others. As stated by one Grahm Greene:

> *"The truth has never been of any real value to any human being - it is a symbol for mathematicians and philosophers to pursue. In human relations kindness and lies are worth a thousand truths."*

That dishonesty is conditioned in us for the sake of others is not to say we do neglect ourselves. On the contrary; so proficient is the human creature at adapting a skill to its own uses that upon the observation of the effectiveness of dishonesty when used for the sake of others it would be an utter disgrace of the human faculties not to utilize such a skill for the sake of the self. To what situation shall we use this newly acquired skill for our own sake? Prior to proper experience we shall (as we often observe) use it without distinction; when necessary and unnecessary. Such a phenomenon again is observable in children as they develop and pass through a stage where they are dishonest incessantly. Due to the ineffectiveness of dishonesty when not necessary and the degradation of the effectiveness of dishonesty when utilized all the time it is observed with proper experience the incessant dishonesty is curtailed to utilization in situations of necessity.

So it is dishonesty is instilled and fostered within individuals. Not from an innate moral nature (*ab intra ingenium*: innate character from within) but from a conditioned ethical compulsion (*ab extra coactum*: compulsion from outside). What of dishonesty to the self; such a thing should serve no purpose as no one is aware of what is expressed in the communion to the self save the self. No ethical purpose is present for the corruption of the moral self so where does moral deception arise from? It is easily observed due to the self bias of an individual they are apt to want to hear that which they desire then what is fact. This predisposition expresses potentiality for effectiveness but does not denote the cause. To surmise the cause in one word the corruption of the self arises from habit. The effectiveness of dishonesty for the sake of others and the self being readily established it is perfectly reasonable to attempt dishonesty to the self for the self. Particularly as we have shown we have a disposition to believe our own dishonesty. So it is stated by one Francios de la Rochfocauld:

> *"We get so much in the habit of wearing disguises before others that we finally appear disguised before ourselves."*

In this manner we have defined the process by which dishonesty becomes a part of humanity. Honesty being the natural state of humanity is always present and readily available for usage. Dishonesty first arising for the sake of others as conditioned by others, followed by dishonesty for the sake of the self out of necessity, all culminating in dishonesty to the self caused by the habit of dishonesty successfully established by dishonesty to others for the sake of others and the self. This section being titled honesty has not disclosed any reason as of yet to be honest. Indeed it would seem the whole of humanity is condemned to live in a dishonest world. However we have disclosed the reasons for ethical and moral honesty in our analysis of dishonesty.

Ethical honesty (*ab extra probitas*) is essential for dishonesty. In order to maximize the effectiveness of dishonesty one must be as honest as possible as much as possible. Indeed one must even be as honest as possible when being dishonest. Honesty is what gives any expression sensicality and sensibility. The more honest something is the more sensical and sensible it is. Such is the assumption which we have made throughout this entire chapter which we now find verified here. To be effectively dishonest one must be perceived as honest even when one is not. To be perceived as honest one must commonly be honest so as to establish familiar trust (*fidelis de vulgaris*). It is often said one need only appear honest to be perceived as honest. We do not simply accept this as mimicry perfectly achieved becomes personification. Thus if one were to mimic honesty to the point they may not be perceived as dishonest than we shall say they no longer mimic, rather they have personally become as honest as any other honest being.

Moral honesty (*ab intra probitas*) is simply human nature. No other reason is required for why one should be morally honest. Just as moral dishonesty arises from a habit of ethical dishonesty we shall see moral honesty arises from a habit of ethical honesty. While such is the case we do observe in order to be ethically dishonest moral honesty is often maintained and present as well. In order to be dishonest one must know the honest expression so as to avoid expressing it. This knowledge of the honest expression is known to the self and communicated to the self and to no other. It is only when dishonesty is exercised to the extent it becomes natural to be dishonest to the self that an individual is at a loss. Not at a loss of what is or what can be done, but at a loss of what they themselves could be. For moral dishonesty accomplishes nothing more than to rob an individual of their potential by placating them to accept what they are rather than encouraging them to endeavor to be what they may become. By means of moral honesty we may improve the self by recognition of our own faults. Moral dishonesty may convince the self there is no need for improvement as perfection maybe viewed where perfection is not present. As expressed by one Tite Kubo in his manga Bleach Chapter 306:

"*Immaculate being was it? In this... existence perfection*

is an illusion regardless of all those who utter the contrary. This is the reality. Common man seeks it out. They aspire to achieve it as if it were some tangible thing. But, the fact of the matter is perfection is a hallow shell. It is devoid of any substance. I spit on perfection. Perfection, afterall, implies you have reached the summit. No trial and error. No ability to conceptualize. An omniscient being would have no need for such superfluous things. Am I making myself clear? For people... such as ourselves, perfection would render us obsolete. Many magnificent things have been and will continue to come into existence. And yet, every last one of them will fall short of perfections finish line. Our function as men... relies on their many short-comings. Then and only then can we apply the fruits of our labor. To put it simply, as soon as you began spouting that nonsense about an immaculate being your fate was sealed. How dare you call yourself a man..."

Conclusion

Now we shall attempt to summarize all we have said in the following chapter. The following assertions have been made:

1.   Explicit Meaning is the agreed upon meaning of a common expression. Also known as a definition for literary term or common conditional response to specific physical stimuli.
2.   Explication is the process by which an explicit meaning is determined based on a common expression utilized for a specific implicit meaning.
3.   Explicit Honesty is the accord of an explicit expression to syntactical, grammatical, and sensical standards established by any given society.
4.   Implicit Meaning is what is intended by an expression or the implied meaning of what is expressed.
5.   Implication is the often improper determination the implicit meaning may be derived from a particular expression and the explicit meaning.
6.   Implicit Honesty is in relation to intention of what is expressed to the effort to express it and is manifested often as sensibility.
7.   The purpose of expression is to convey the moral (internal) self to either the self or to that which is not the self.
8.   The Explicit Recipient is any one able to perceive and comprehend the explicit expression. It must consist of at least one person. Unintended explicit recipients are acceptable though not desired.
9.   The Implicit Recipient is the person or persons in-

tended to receive the implied meaning of an expression. While there must always be at minimum a single explicit recipient often times there is no implicit recipient. Unintended implicit recipients are not acceptable or desired.

10. The Intent of an Expression is determined by the relation of the explicit to implicit recipient and explicit to the implicit meaning. So long as the explicit and implicit recipients are the same; and the explicit and implicit meanings are in accordance with one another then the intent of the expression is honest.

11. Should inequality occur between explicit and implicit recipients than the expression seeks to deceive another and is to be termed ethically deceitful, in which the desire is to convey the self to one but not to another.

12. Should inequality occur between explicit and implicit meanings than the expression is to hide the self from the self or another and is to be termed morally deceptive, in which the desire is simply to conceal the self from either the self or another.

13. Misunderstanding occurs as either misapprehension or misconstruction. The former is to intend to understand and fail to do so and is manifested as simply not understanding. The latter is to intentionally misunderstand so as to glorify the self and is manifested as a form of pride, perversion, or piousness.

14. The effectiveness of Ethical Deceit and Moral Deception is grounded firmly in individual self biased expressed as confidence in ones own knowledge of the world, those are to be trusted, and those to trust.

15. All expressions have an intention as honest or dishonest, which by means of context are meant to be true or false. Reality is the measure by which any expression is determined as true or false whether hon-

est or dishonest.

16.   Honesty is human nature. Ethical Deceit is instilled in childhood for the sake of others, Ethical Deceit is developed by practice for the sake of the self, and finally Moral Deception utilized against the self out of habit of ethically deceiving others.

17.   Ethical Honesty is essential to maximize the effectiveness of Ethical Deceit. Perfect pretense of honesty becomes the personification of honesty.

18.   Moral Honesty is simply human nature. While not manifested it is never absent as the very subject of honesty and dishonesty hinge on human ability to be dishonest. A skill which is made possible only by our conscious or unconscious understanding of moral honesty.

So we conclude our explanation and argument regarding the subjects of honesty, ethical deceit, and moral deception. The utilization of deceit is necessary for human interaction. Deception is a resultant condition of the deceit we utilize with others. Nonetheless it may not be denied honesty is our nature. Honest we would be if it were not for the sake of the rest of humanity. We all wish to speak the truth though there are few if any of us who would like to hear the truth. Thus do we speak in numerous manners which are not true though they incorporate truth within them, all for the sake of society, life, and happiness; as stated by Michel de Montaigne and Carlos Castaneda:

> *"If falsehood, like truth, had but one face, we would be more on equal terms. For we would consider the contrary of what the liar said to be certain. But the opposite of truth has a hundred thousand faces and an infinite field."*

> *"It's better to get something worthwhile done using deception than to fail to get something worthwhile done using truth."*